Already There

Short stories for souls who
forgot they don't need fixing

Published by Inner **Sea Journeys**
ISBN: 979-8-9995979-1-5

Disclaimer: This book is intended for informational and educational purposes only. It offers insights and strategies for personal growth and self-improvement, but is *not a substitute for professional medical, psychological, or psychiatric advice, diagnosis, or treatment.* If you are experiencing mental health challenges, please consult a qualified healthcare provider. The author and publisher disclaim any liability for any loss or risk incurred directly or indirectly from the use of the information **contained herein.**

For Lily

*You are **my why.***

Table of Contents

Preface

Self-knowledge shouldn't feel **like homework.**

You wouldn't ruin a good novel with a highlighter and a study guide, would you? Dissecting every page until the joy **leaked out?**
You'd just read it and let it change you without trying. Get lost in it.
Let **it unfold.**

Why can't getting to know yourself work the **same way?**

These stories are designed to help you remember what you already know, without the usual assignments that come with personal growth. No journals. No steps. No pressure. No becoming a better version **of yourself.**

You're already interesting. You already have main **character energy.** You just forgot. Don't worry, you'll **get it.**

~ Hanna

The Forgetting Game

A Mental Jujitsu Move

....

As taught by Master Wei, who claimed to be 847 years old, but looked suspiciously like he might be making that up, at the School for Advanced Forgetting, located somewhere between Where-You-Think-You-Are and Where-You-Actually-Are.

....

"Sit," said Master Wei, patting a cushion that looked like it had been sat on by roughly a thousand students before you. "Or stand. Or do that thing humans do where they're sitting, but also fidgeting. Doesn't matter. The forgetting works in **all positions."**

You settled onto the cushion, which was surprisingly comfortable despite its apparent age. Master Wei himself looked ageless in the way that very old trees do: weathered but sturdy, with eyes that twinkled like he knew a joke he wasn't quite ready **to tell.**

"You have come," he said, settling into his own cushion with the fluid grace of someone who had made peace with gravity, "to learn the art of remembering. But this is backwards thinking, like trying to catch water with a net. Today, we learn the art of forgetting, which is much more useful and significantly less exhausting."

He pulled out what appeared to be an ancient scroll, unrolled it dramatically, then paused and chuckled. "Oh, this is my grocery list. Soy sauce, rice, more tea..." He rolled it back up. "Good thing I forgot to bring the right scroll. Makes this more authentic. The best teachings, they don't come from scrolls anyway. They come from forgetting you need scrolls."

Round One: The Worry Archaeology Dig

"First exercise," Master Wei announced, rubbing his hands together like a child about to play a particularly delightful game. "I want you to remember—and this is very important—what you were worried about exactly one year ago today."

You closed your eyes and tried to reach back into the archives of your anxiety. One year ago... what had been keeping you up at night? What crisis had seemed so urgent, so important, so worthy of your precious worry?

"Take your time," Master Wei said kindly. "Really dig around in there. What was the big catastrophe you were preparing for? What terrible thing was definitely going to happen? What problem was so serious you spent weeks thinking about it?"

You searched your memory, expecting to find a catalog of disasters, but instead find... vague impressions. Something about work, maybe? A relationship issue that seemed important at the time? The harder you tried to remember the specific details of your year-old worries, the more they seemed to slip away **like smoke.**

"Ah," said Master Wei, noticing your expression. "You are beginning to see. The mind, it is like a very efficient janitor. It throws away the old worries to make room for the new ones. Very practical, this janitor mind. Doesn't ask permission, just—" He made a sweeping **gesture. "Gone!"**

You opened your eyes, slightly disturbed by how difficult it was to recall anxieties that had once felt monumentally important.

"Now here comes the jujitsu part," Master Wei said, his eyes definitely twinkling now. "If your mind threw away last year's worries—worries that felt very real and very serious at the time—what does this tell you about this year's worries?"

The question hung in the air like incense, sweet and slightly disorienting.

"Your homework brain, it is saying 'But this year's worries are different! This year's worries are real!'" Master Wei chuckled. "This is what last year's brain said too. Very consistent, this homework brain. Always thinks its current worries are the first worries **that matter."**

Round Two: The Embarrassment **Treasure Hunt**

"Second exercise," Master Wei said, producing what looked like a small bell from his pocket and ringing it once. "Think back to your most embarrassing moment from middle school. The one that made you want to disappear into the floor. The one you were sure everyone would **remember forever.**"

This was easier to access. You could feel your face getting warm as you recalled... actually, which embarrassing moment? There had been several that had felt world-ending at the time. The time you tripped in front of your crush? The time you gave the wrong answer in class? The **time you...**

"Found one?" Master Wei asked. "Good. Now, important question: How many people from your middle school have mentioned this embarrassing moment to you in the past **five years?**"

You thought about it. How many people had brought up your middle school disasters recently? How many of your classmates had you even seen in recent years? How many of them even remembered you at all, let alone your specific moments **of mortification?**

"Zero," you **said, surprised.**

"Exactly zero!" Master Wei clapped his hands with delight. "Your thirteen-year-old brain was convinced everyone would remember your embarrassment forever. Your thirteen-year-old brain was wrong. Very dramatically wrong. Like, embarrassingly wrong **about embarrassment!**"

He laughed at his own joke, which somehow made it funnier.

"But here is the beautiful part," he continued. "Your brain has not learned from this mistake. Right now, today, your adult brain is worrying about looking foolish in front of people who will forget whatever foolish thing you do approximately ten minutes after you do it. Maybe less if something interesting happens on their phones."

Round Three: The Problem That Solved Itself

"Third exercise," Master Wei said, now producing what appeared to be a rubber duck from his other pocket. "Tell me about a problem you had two years ago that you were absolutely certain would require enormous effort to solve. Something that kept you up at night, making plans and strategies and backup plans for the backup plans."

You thought back two years. There had been that situation at work... or maybe the thing with your living situation... or that relationship drama that had seemed so complex and urgent...

"Got one?" Master Wei asked, making the rubber duck nod encouragingly. "Good. Now tell me: how did you solve it?"

You tried to remember the elaborate solution you'd implemented, the careful strategy you'd deployed, the massive effort you'd put forth to resolve the crisis. But as you traced back through your memory, you realized something odd.

"I... I'm not sure I actually did anything specific to solve it," you said slowly. "It just kind of... **resolved itself?**"

"Aha!" Master Wei exclaimed, making the rubber duck do a little victory dance. "The duck agrees! This is the secret that problems don't want you to know: most of them solve themselves if you stop poking them with **worry sticks.**"

He set the duck down on his cushion where it seemed to watch the proceedings with its small, **plastic eyes.**

"Your problem-solving brain, it wants to take credit for everything good that happens. But truth is, life is very good at untangling itself. Like string in a pocket—leave it alone, it sorts itself out. Keep messing with it, you make knots that weren't there before."

Round Four: The Temporary **Permanent Crisis**

"Fourth exercise," Master Wei announced, now pulling out what looked like a small hourglass filled with glitter instead of sand. "Think of something that happened in your life that felt absolutely permanent. Something that made you think 'This is it, everything has changed forever, nothing will ever be **the same.'**"

This was easy. You'd had several moments like that: breakups that felt like the end of the world, job losses that seemed catastrophic, changes that appeared to have permanently altered the course of **your life.**

"But wait," Master Wei said, turning the glitter hourglass upside down and watching the sparkles fall slowly to the other side. "Look around you right now. Are you still in that **permanent situation?** Is everything still exactly as changed as it felt it would **be forever?**"

You looked around the meditation room, then at your own life. The "permanent" crisis you'd been thinking of... you were no longer in it. Somehow, without noticing exactly when or how, you'd moved through it. What had felt like a fundamental shift in the nature of reality had turned out to be more like weather—dramatic while it was happening, but **ultimately temporary.**

"Everything is temporary," Master Wei said gently, watching the glitter settle. "The good things, the bad things, the medium things, the things that feel like they're made of concrete, but are actually made of clouds. Even this conversation is temporary. Very sad, but also **very liberating.**"

He turned the hourglass again, and the glitter began its slow dance back to the **other side.**

"Permanent is just temporary that hasn't **finished yet.**"

Round Five: The Memory Hole of **Infinite Suffering**

"Fifth exercise," Master Wei said, producing what appeared to be a snow globe from yet another pocket. How many pockets did this man have? "This one is advanced forgetting. Are you ready for advanced forgetting?"

You nodded, curious about what could be more advanced than forgetting your **own problems.**

"Try to remember the exact feeling of the worst physical pain you've ever experienced. Not the fact that it happened, not the story about it, but the actual **sensation itself.**"

You thought back to your worst injury, your most painful illness, that time you... but as you tried to recall the precise feeling, you found you couldn't. You could remember that it had hurt, remember that it had been terrible, remember the circumstances around it, but the actual physical sensation was gone, filed away **somewhere inaccessible.**

"Interesting, yes?" Master Wei shook the snow globe, and tiny glitter particles swirled around a miniature mountain. "Your body, it has a delete function for pain. Very wise, this body. Imagine if you could still feel every hurt from your entire life, all at the same time. You would never get out of bed."

The snow in the globe settled slowly, creating a **peaceful scene.**

"But your mind, it does not have such good delete function for emotional pain. Your mind keeps old hurts fresh, like flowers in a refrigerator. Very inefficient. This is why we practice forgetting— to help the mind learn what the body already knows."

Round Six: The Future **Worry Preview**

"Sixth exercise," Master Wei said, now pulling out what looked like a Magic 8-Ball, except instead of answers, it seemed to show swirling clouds. "This is time travel exercise. Very advanced. We go forward instead **of backward.**"

He held up the cloudy sphere and gazed into it with mock seriousness.

"Imagine it is one year from now. You are sitting with a friend, and they ask you 'What were you worried about this time last year?' That means they're asking about right now, today, this moment. What will you **tell them?**"

You tried to project forward, to imagine yourself a year from now attempting to remember today's anxieties. The exercise felt strange, like trying to remember something that hadn't **happened yet.**

"Can you see yourself struggling to remember what today's big worry was?" Master Wei asked, peering into the cloudy ball. "Can you see yourself laughing a little at how serious it seemed at **the time?** Can you see yourself saying 'Oh, that old thing? It worked itself **out somehow'?**"

The image was surprisingly clear. Future-you, relaxed and probably dealing with completely different concerns, trying to recall why present-you was so worked up about things that future-you could **barely remember.**

"Ah, you see it!" Master Wei smiled. "This is the secret: your future self is very bad at remembering your current self's problems. Your future self is too busy living in the future to maintain a proper archive of old worries. Very unreliable, this **future self.**"

Round Seven: The Dramatic **Importance Illusion**

"Seventh exercise," Master Wei announced, **producing what** appeared to be a pair of reading glasses, except the lenses seemed to be made of soap bubbles. "Put these on. No, don't actually put them on, they're imaginary. **Just pretend.**"

You mimed putting on the **bubble glasses.**

"These are called Perspective Glasses. Very expensive, very rare. Through these glasses, you can see how important your problems look to **the universe.**"

You looked around the room through your imaginary glasses, and Master Wei **gestured grandly.**

"What do you see? How does your current biggest worry look when viewed from the perspective of the galaxy? How about from the perspective of the ocean? How about from the perspective of your cat, who is probably asleep right now and has never worried about anything more complex than whether the food bowl is **adequately full?**"

Through the imaginary bubble lenses, your problems seemed to shrink. Not disappear—they were still there—but they looked less like towering mountains and more like small hills. Still real, still present, but somehow more manageable when viewed from a **wider angle.**

"Problems are like balloons," Master Wei said, taking off his own imaginary glasses. "Very big when you hold them close to your face, normal size when you hold them at arm's length. The problem doesn't change size; your distance from it **changes size.**"

Round Eight: The **Suffering Olympics**

"Eighth exercise," Master Wei said, pulling out what looked like a small trophy made of tin foil. "This is very serious exercise. We compete in the Suffering Olympics. Winner gets this lovely trophy."

He held up the makeshift trophy, which caught the light and somehow managed to look both ridiculous **and precious.**

"Rules are simple: I describe a category of suffering, you try to remember if you have ever experienced this type of suffering, and if you have, you win a point. Ready?"

You nodded, unsure where this **was going.**

"Category One: Suffering About Things That **Never Happened.** Have you ever spent significant time worrying about events that never **actually occurred?**"

You raised your hand sheepishly. About 90% of your worries fell into this category.

"One point! Category Two: Suffering About Things You Cannot Control. Have you ever been upset about weather, other people's opinions, or the general state of the world?"

Another raised hand. This was becoming embarrassing.

"Two points! Category Three: Suffering About Suffering. Have you ever been worried about being worried, or anxious about being anxious, or stressed about being stressed?"

You raised your hand again, now laughing despite yourself.

"Three points! Congratulations!" Master Wei handed you the tin foil trophy with great ceremony. "You have achieved the highest possible score in the Suffering Olympics. You are a champion sufferer!"

You held the silly trophy, and somehow it felt both absurd and meaningful.

"But here is the secret about the Suffering Olympics," Master Wei whispered conspiratorially. "Everyone who plays gets the same score. Everyone wins the same trophy. Because suffering about imaginary things, uncontrollable things, and suffering itself is the human condition. You are not special for doing it, and you are not broken for doing it. You are just... human."

Round Nine: The Memory Palace of Things That Don't Matter

"Ninth exercise," Master Wei said, standing up and stretching like a cat in a sunbeam. "We take a tour of your Memory Palace. But not the important rooms—the rooms where you keep things that don't **matter anymore.**"

He began walking around the room as if touring an invisible mansion.

"Here is the room where you keep all the times people were rude to you in grocery stores. Very spacious room, yes? And over here, the room where you store all the times you said something awkward at parties. Oh, and this wing is dedicated to all the times you were convinced you were going to be late, but then **you weren't.**"

You followed him on the imaginary tour, amazed at how much mental real estate you'd apparently devoted to **forgettable moments.**

"And here," Master Wei said, opening an invisible door with a flourish, "is the room where you keep all the days you wasted worrying about things that turned out fine. This is the biggest room in the palace. Has its own **zip code.**"

The invisible tour was starting to feel very real, and slightly overwhelming.

"Now," Master Wei said, pulling out an imaginary match, "we burn it **all down.**"

He mimed striking the match and tossing it into the **invisible room.**

"Don't worry," he said, noticing your expression. "Memory palaces are fireproof when you're burning things that don't matter. Only the important stuff survives. And you might be surprised how little of it there **actually is.**"

Round Ten: The Reverse **Gratitude Practice**

"Tenth exercise," Master Wei announced, settling back onto his cushion. "This is called Reverse Gratitude. Instead of being grateful for what you have, you are grateful for what you don't have **to remember.**"

He pulled out what appeared to be a notebook made of clouds. You couldn't quite tell if it was real or another **pocket illusion.**

"For example," he said, pretending to write in the cloud notebook, "I am grateful I don't remember every mosquito bite I've ever gotten. I am grateful I don't remember every time I've been stuck in traffic. I am grateful I don't remember every bad song I've **ever heard.**"

The exercise felt strange, but **oddly liberating.**

"Your turn," he said, offering you the cloud notebook. "What are you grateful to **have forgotten?**"

You took the notebook (which felt like holding solidified air) and began to list things you were glad not to remember: every headache, every time you'd been disappointed by weather, every commercial you'd ever been forced to watch, every moment of boredom, every minor frustration...

"Good!" Master Wei nodded approvingly. "You see? Your brain is constantly doing you favors by forgetting the forgettable. But it doesn't get credit for this excellent service. Very underappreciated, this forgetting brain."

Round Eleven: The Time Zoom Function

"Eleventh exercise," Master Wei said, producing what looked like a telescope made of bamboo and rainbow-colored glass. "This is the Time Zoom. Very powerful instrument. Can see far into past and future."

He handed you the telescope, which was surprisingly light.

"First, zoom in very close to right now. What do you see? What are you worried about in this exact moment?"

You peered through the telescope at the present moment. Your current concerns filled the entire view—work stress, relationship questions, financial worries, health anxieties.

"Now," Master Wei instructed, "zoom out to this week. How big are those worries now?"

You adjusted the imaginary telescope. The problems were still there, but they seemed smaller, part of a larger pattern of days and activities.

"Now zoom out to this month. Now this year. Now this decade."

With each zoom level, your current worries became smaller and smaller, until they were just tiny dots in a vast landscape of time. Not gone, but proportional.

"And now," Master Wei said, "the ultimate zoom. Pull back to see your entire life from beginning to end, like a movie viewed from space."

From this perspective, your current problems weren't just small—they were brief. Temporary fluctuations in a much longer story. You could see how you'd worried before, how those worries had resolved or been forgotten, how you'd moved through cycles of concern and relief and concern again.

"This is the true perspective," Master Wei said gently. "Not that your problems don't matter, but that they matter temporarily. They are chapters, not the whole book."

Round Twelve: The Worry Warranty

"Twelfth exercise," Master Wei announced, pulling out what appeared to be an official-looking document with a red seal. "This is advanced business. We examine the warranty on your worries."

He unrolled the document with **great ceremony.**

"According to this warranty," he read in an official-sounding voice, "your worries are guaranteed to be 95% useless, with a money-back guarantee if they actually prevent the problems you're **worried about."**

He looked at you over **the document.**

"Have you ever had a worry that actually prevented the thing you were worried about? Like, has worrying about being late ever made you less late? Has worrying about making mistakes ever made you **less mistake-prone?"**

You thought about it. Had worry ever actually functioned as problem prevention? Or was it just… mental activity that felt important, but **accomplished nothing?**

"Worry comes with lifetime warranty," Master Wei continued, "but warranty only covers creating more worry. Very limited warranty. Does not cover: solving problems, preventing disasters, making things better, or being useful in any **practical way."**

He rolled up **the document.**

"But here is the good news: you can return worry anytime, no receipt required. Universe has very generous return policy on useless **mental activities."**

The Final Round: The **Forgetting Graduation**

"Final exercise," Master Wei said, standing up and bowing deeply. "This is graduation ceremony. You ready to graduate from the School for **Advanced Forgetting?**"

You nodded, though you weren't entirely sure what you were **graduating into.**

"For your final exam," he said, "I want you to try to remember everything we've talked about today. Every exercise, every insight, every moment **of clarity.**"

You tried to hold onto all the lessons, all the realizations, all the techniques for letting go. But even as you grasped for them, they seemed to slip away, leaving only impressions and feelings rather than **concrete methods.**

"Ah," Master Wei smiled, "you are failing the test perfectly. This is excellent failing. You see? Even the method for forgetting your problems can be forgotten. Even the techniques for letting go can be **let go.**"

He placed a hand on **your shoulder.**

"The best teachings work like medicine: they cure the disease and then disappear from the body. You don't need to remember how to forget. Forgetting knows how to do itself. You just need to stop interfering with **the process.**"

The Non-Homework Assignment

"Now," Master Wei said, walking you toward a door that definitely hadn't been there when you arrived, "I give you homework. But this is very special homework that you **cannot do.**"

He handed you a piece of paper that appeared to **be blank.**

"Your assignment is to not worry about anything for **the next** twenty-four hours. But if you try to not worry, you will worry about not worrying. So you cannot try to do this homework. You can only fail at it, which is the only way **to succeed.**"

You stared at the blank paper, trying to understand **the logic.**

"If you find yourself worrying tomorrow," Master **Wei advised,** "remember that you are supposed to fail at not worrying, so worrying means you are succeeding at failing, which means you are doing the **homework correctly.**"

Your head was starting to hurt from the **circular logic.**

"And if you don't worry tomorrow, then you have failed at failing, which means you have succeeded without trying, which is the highest form of success and also means you have done the **homework correctly.**"

He opened the door, revealing the ordinary **world outside.**

"Either way, you cannot do this wrong. Very good homework design. Even if you forget the homework completely, you will have succeeded at forgetting, which was the point **all along.**"

The Epilogue That Wasn't Supposed to Be Remembered

Master Wei walked you to the threshold between the School for Advanced Forgetting and the regular world where people remember things **on purpose.**

"One last thing," he said. "The biggest secret about forgetting: you cannot force it. Forgetting is like sleep: the harder you try, the more awake you become. Forgetting happens when you stop trying to remember and stop trying **to forget.**"

He looked at you with those **twinkling eyes.**

"In fact, the best thing you can do right now is try to remember everything I've taught you. Try very hard. Make lists. **Take notes.** Set reminders. Worry about forgetting the lessons **about forgetting.**"

You looked at him suspiciously. This felt like **another trap.**

"Because," he continued, grinning now, "the harder you try to remember the method for forgetting your problems, the more you will forget to have the problems in the first place. Very sneaky, this forgetting. Works even when you're trying to **prevent it.**"

He stepped back and began to close **the door.**

"Oh, and one more thing," he called through the closing gap.
"If anyone asks you what you learned today, just tell them you forgot.
They will think you are being modest, but you will know you are
being accurate."

The door closed with a soft click, leaving you standing on the
sidewalk with a blank piece of paper and the distinct feeling that
something important had just happened, though you couldn't quite
remember what.

As you walked home, you tried to recall the specific exercises, the
exact insights, the precise techniques Master Wei had taught you.
But the harder you grasped for them, the more they seemed to slip
away, leaving behind only a lightness in your chest and the strange
sensation that you'd been carrying something heavy for a long time
and had just set **it down.**

By the time you reached your front door, you could barely remember
what you'd been worried about that morning. The problems were
still there, technically, but they felt distant somehow, like clouds
on the horizon that might bring rain later but weren't bothering
anyone **right now.**

You looked at the blank paper in your hand. For a moment, you
considered writing down everything you could remember from
the lesson, but then you realized that would defeat the purpose.
Instead, you folded the paper into an origami crane and placed

it on your windowsill, where it could catch the light and remind you of something you weren't supposed to **remember anyway.**

Later that evening, a friend called and asked how your day **had been.**

"I went to this class," you said, "but I forgot what it **was about.**"

"That's too bad," your friend said. "Was **it important?**"

You looked at the paper crane on your windowsill **and smiled.**

"I don't think so," you said. "In fact, I think that was **the point.**"

Post-Credits Scene: Master **Wei's Secret**

Long after you'd left, Master Wei sat in his meditation room, chuckling to himself and putting his various pocket **items away.** The rubber duck, the snow globe, the tin foil trophy—all of them went into a simple cardboard box labeled "Teaching Props for People Who Need Props to Learn Things They **Already Know.**"

He pulled out his phone (which was decidedly modern and un-mystical) and sent a text to his colleague: "Another one forgot successfully. The forgetting technique is **working perfectly.**"

The response came quickly: "How do you know **it's working?**"

Master Wei typed back: "Because they stopped trying to remember how to be happy and just started being happy instead. Ancient technique, very effective. I learned it from my grandmother, who learned it from **her cat.**"

He put the phone away and looked around the room, which was actually just a rented space in a community center. Tomorrow there would be a knitting circle here, and next week a support group for people afraid **of butterflies.**

But for now, it was the School for Advanced Forgetting, and somewhere in the city, another person was discovering that the best way to solve problems is often to forget to have them in the **first place.**

Master Wei—whose real name was actually Gary, and who had learned everything he knew about forgetting from successfully forgetting most of what he'd learned in graduate psychology programs—smiled and turned off **the lights.**

The forgetting game was working exactly as intended: by teaching people to lose, **they won.**

And the best part was, by tomorrow most of them would forget how they'd learned to forget, which meant they'd be using the technique without knowing they were **using it.**

Which was, Gary reflected as he locked up the community center, exactly how all the best techniques worked.

....

*Author's Note: This story works by using the brain's natural tendency to forget against its own tendency to dramatize problems. By pointing out what we've already forgotten, it reveals the temporary nature of most suffering. The playful, paradoxical instructions create a kind of mental jujitsu where trying to remember becomes a way of forgetting, and failing to retain the lessons becomes a way of succeeding at **letting go**.*

*The wisdom is delivered through humor and circular logic specifically because the rational mind can't argue with something it can't quite grasp, allowing the insights to slip past psychological defenses and work at a **deeper level**.*

*If you remember nothing else from this story, you have learned everything it was meant **to teach**.*

The God Who Quit

A Blasphemous Bedtime Story

On a Tuesday that felt like every other Tuesday since the beginning of time, God woke up tired.

Not the kind of tired that comes from staying up too late binge-watching the cosmos unfold, but the bone-deep exhaustion that settles into your divine essence when you've been micromanaging infinity for longer than anyone should reasonably be expected to do. Even if you're omnipotent. Especially, if **you're omnipotent.**

God stretched, and somewhere in the Andromeda Galaxy, a supernova flickered in response. A headache was forming behind divine eyes—the kind that comes from simultaneously tracking the flight path of every sparrow, while also ensuring that quantum mechanics continued to make absolutely no sense to mortals, just **as intended.**

"Right," God muttered, scratching what might have been a beard or might have been a nebula, depending on your perspective. "Today's agenda."

The list materialized in the air, written in letters of pure light that hurt to look at directly:

- Maintain gravitational constants across 2.3 trillion galaxies

- Resolve prayer backlog (847,293,722,418 and climbing)

- Fix that thing with the platypus (seriously, what was I thinking?)

- Supervise continental drift (Pacific Plate is getting uppity again)

- Monitor free will vs. predestination paradox (ongoing crisis)

- Ensure proper rotation of Earth (humans get cranky when days are uneven)

- Update laws of physics (someone figured out how to make toast fall butter-side up)

- Individual guardian angel assignments (3.2 billion new births this month)

- Quality control on sunsets (complaints about "lack of artistic vision" in Nebraska)

- Microscopic oversight of every subatomic particle in existence

- And approximately 8.7 octillion other tasks

God stared at the list. The list stared back, somehow managing to look smug despite being made of pure energy.

"You know what?" God said to no one in particular, because when you're omnipresent, you're always talking to yourself anyway. "I quit."

The words hung in the cosmic void for exactly 3.7 seconds before reality had a minor panic attack.

The Angel of Bureaucracy, a being so devoted to procedure that it had evolved seventeen different forms of filing systems, materialized instantly. Its many eyes blinked in synchronized horror.

"Sir! Ma'am! Your Divine Unpronounceable Name! You can't just quit! The universe requires constant supervision! The mortals need guidance! The laws of physics won't enforce themselves!"

God was already walking away, leaving footprints in the fabric of spacetime. "Watch me."

"But Sir! The sparrows! Who will note their falling?"

"They'll figure it out."

"The prayers! The supplications! The desperate midnight bargains!"

"They've got voicemail."

"The very foundations of reality will crumble!"

God paused, turned around, and smiled. It was the kind of smile that contained the warmth of a billion suns and the mischief of a child who had just discovered they could make farting noises with their armpit.

"Will they, though?"

And with that, God walked to the edge of existence, pulled out a hammock that materialized from pure possibility, strung it between two pillars of crystallized time, and lay down.

The universe held its breath.

God closed infinite eyes and sighed, a sound like wind through autumn leaves, like the last note of a song you can't quite remember, like the space between heartbeats when you're falling asleep.

"It's already done," God whispered.

....

On Earth, Margaret Helsing was having the worst day of her life. Her alarm hadn't gone off, her coffee maker had exploded (literally exploded, filling her kitchen with what appeared to be caffeinated shrapnel), her car wouldn't start, and her phone had somehow developed the ability to only receive calls from telemarketers speaking in ancient Sumerian.

She stood in her driveway, looking up at the sky with the particular expression humans get when they're about to have a serious conversation with the universe.

"Really?" she called out. "Today? Of all days? I have the Henderson presentation, my mother's birthday dinner, and I haven't even figured out what to do about Jerry yet, and you **decide to—**"

She paused. Something **was different.**

The sky was still blue. The sun was still doing its sun thing. Birds were still birding. But there was something... absent. Like when you're listening to music and suddenly realize the bass line has stopped, and you didn't notice exactly when, but now there's this hollow space where something used to be.

Margaret looked around more carefully. Mrs. Chen was still watering her roses next door, but she was smiling. Actually smiling. Mrs. Chen, who had perfected the art of disapproving of everything from cloud formations to the way people walked, was humming.

Down the street, the Kowalski twins—those twin tornadoes of destruction who had made it their life's mission to terrorize every living thing within a three-block radius—were sitting quietly on their front steps, sharing a juice box and actually having what appeared to be a conversation rather than their usual routine of seeing who could scream the loudest.

Something was **definitely wrong.**

Or maybe, Margaret thought as she watched Mr. Patterson's ancient, arthritic dog suddenly leap a fence it hadn't been able to jump in five years, something was **finally right.**

Her phone buzzed. For the first time all day, it wasn't a telemarketer. It was **her boss.**

"Henderson presentation's been moved to next week," the text read. "Client decided they needed more time to think. Also, I'm giving everyone the afternoon off. Beautiful day, **isn't it?**"

Margaret stared at her phone. Her boss, Janet, was many things— efficient, demanding, capable of turning a quarterly report into a weapon of mass destruction—but she had never, in the seven years Margaret had worked for her, noticed weather that wasn't actively trying to **kill someone.**

Margaret's car chose that moment to start on the first try, purring like a contented cat instead of making its usual sounds of mechanical death.

"Okay," she said to the universe. "What's **the catch?**"

The universe, having recently been abandoned by its primary administrator, had no comment.

· ·

In the cosmic hammock, God was discovering the simple pleasure of not having to think about everything all at once. For the first time in, well, forever, divine attention wasn't split between monitoring the precise temperature needed for stellar fusion while simultaneously ensuring that every coin flip everywhere had the appropriate **randomness quotient.**

Instead, God was watching a single leaf fall from a tree on a planet in a galaxy whose name was mostly **unpronounceable consonants.**

The leaf fell in a gentle spiral, caught an updraft, performed a small pirouette, and landed softly on the nose of a sleeping cat. The cat opened one eye, regarded the leaf with the philosophical acceptance that only cats possess, and went back to sleep.

It **was perfect.**

God had forgotten that individual moments could be perfect. When you're managing infinity, you miss the small things. The way light catches in a raindrop. The exact moment when bread becomes toast. The precise angle of a dog's head when it's trying to understand **human behavior.**

"Sir?" The Angel of Bureaucracy had found the hammock and was hovering nearby, clutching a clipboard that appeared to be on fire. "The situation is becoming... unusual."

"How so?"

"Well, without your direct supervision, things **are... working.**"

God cracked open one eye. **"Define 'working.'"**

"The mortals are... I'm not sure how to put this... they're being kind to each other. Without instruction. Without commandments. Without threats of eternal damnation or promises of paradise. They're just... **doing it.**"

"Huh."

"In Mumbai, a traffic jam that should have taken three hours to resolve cleared up in twenty minutes, because everyone just started letting each other merge. No one can explain why."

"Interesting."

"In Detroit, a man named Marcus found a wallet with eight hundred dollars in it and not only returned it, but also helped the owner, an elderly woman named Rose, carry her groceries home. She invited him for dinner. He accepted. They're now planning to start a community garden together."

"Good **for them.**"

"Sir, a child in Stockholm dropped her ice cream cone, and instead of crying, she laughed and said, 'I guess that's what the ants were hoping for today.' The ants formed a little procession and carried it away. The child clapped."

God smiled without opening divine eyes. "Kids **get it.**"

"The prayer backlog is... well, it's still growing, but the prayers are changing. Instead of asking for things, people are saying 'thank you.' Thank you for sunlight. Thank you for the fact that water is wet. Thank you for the way cats purr. Thank you for the existence of cookies."

"As it **should be.**"

The Angel of Bureaucracy's seventeen filing systems were all having nervous breakdowns simultaneously. "But Sir! What about the laws of physics? What about entropy? What about the fundamental forces that hold **reality together?**"

God finally opened both eyes and looked at the angel with something that wasn't quite pity, but wasn't quite **amusement either.**

"What **about them?**"

"Well... they're... they're just... running themselves. The strong nuclear force is maintaining atomic cohesion without supervision. Gravity is keeping planets in orbit without micromanagement. Even quantum mechanics is behaving itself, which is frankly unprecedented."

"Maybe," God said gently, "they always were."

....

Back on Earth, things were getting **wonderfully weird.**

In Tokyo, a businessman named Hiroshi was rushing to catch his train when he noticed an old woman struggling with a heavy bag. Without thinking, he stopped to help her. This made him miss his train. Instead of being upset, he found himself oddly relieved. He used the extra time to buy coffee from a vendor he'd walked past every day for three years but had never stopped to talk to. The vendor, it turned out, was a retired philosophy professor who had some fascinating thoughts about the nature **of time.**

Hiroshi arrived at work forty-five minutes late and completely relaxed for the first time in months. His presentation went better than it had any right to. His boss, instead of being angry about the lateness, asked him what he'd done differently, because he seemed **so centered.**

In São Paulo, a woman named Carmen was sitting in traffic that wasn't moving when she looked over and saw the driver in the next car crying. Without thinking, she rolled down her window and asked if he was okay. His name was Eduardo, and he'd just gotten devastating news about his father's health. Carmen, who didn't know Eduardo and had no reason to care, found herself parking her car and sitting with him on the side of the road until he felt ready to **drive again.**

The traffic didn't move any faster, but somehow no one seemed **to mind.**

In Lagos, a street vendor named Adunni gave a mango to a child who couldn't afford it. The child's mother, seeing this kindness, bought three mangoes she didn't need. The man behind her, witnessing this exchange, bought five. By the end of the day, Adunni had sold more mangoes than she ever had, and she spent the profits buying school supplies for children in her neighborhood.

Nobody planned it. Nobody organized it. Nobody commanded it from on high.

It **just happened.**

In the hammock, God was learning to relax. It was harder than it looked. When you've been hypervigilant about every subatomic particle for all of eternity, learning to just let things be requires a kind of courage that even omnipotence doesn't automatically grant.

The Angel of Bureaucracy was still there, still panicking, still occasionally catching fire from **the stress.**

"Sir, I have to report that the situation is escalating. The mortals are... they're figuring **things out.**"

"Such as?"

"A group of scientists in Geneva just solved the unified field theory, but instead of publishing it for fame and glory, they've decided to sit on it until they can figure out how to share it in a way that benefits everyone. They're having tea and discussing ethics."

"Shocking."

"A corporation in New York was about to dump toxic waste into a river, but the CEO's daughter asked him why he was going to poison the fish. He couldn't come up with a good answer, so he didn't do it. The cleanup is costing millions, but he says he sleeps better at night."

"Imagine that."

"Sir, people are... they're starting to realize they don't need to be managed. They're making good choices just because they're good choices. They're being kind just because kindness feels better than cruelty. They're helping each other just because they're all in this together."

God was quiet for a long moment, listening to the sound of existence humming along without divine intervention. Somewhere, a child was learning to ride a bicycle and discovering the joy of forward momentum. Somewhere else, an elderly couple was sitting on a porch, holding hands and not talking, just being present with each other. Somewhere further away, in a galaxy that wasn't even on most cosmic maps, two gas giants were performing an orbital dance that would have made Bach weep with joy.

All of it happening **without supervision.**
All of it perfect in **its imperfection.**
All of it exactly as it **should be.**

"You know what the real blasphemy is?" God **said finally.**

The Angel of Bureaucracy, who had been expecting lightning bolts and divine wrath, was caught off **guard.** "Sir?"

"The blasphemy is thinking that any of this needed to be managed in the first place."

....

Margaret Helsing was having the best day of her life, and she couldn't figure out why.

Everything that had gone wrong in the morning had somehow led to everything going right in the afternoon. The exploded coffee maker had resulted in her neighbor, Mrs. Chen, inviting her over for tea and telling her stories about growing up in Shanghai. The car that wouldn't start had led to her walking to work and discovering a shortcut through a park she'd never noticed, where she'd watched a man teaching his daughter to fly a kite.

The Henderson presentation being postponed had given her time to actually think about what she wanted to say instead of just rushing through slides. When she finally gave it the following week, it was the best presentation of **her career.**

But the real change wasn't in the external circumstances. It was in Margaret herself. She'd stopped waiting for the other shoe to drop. She'd stopped bracing for disaster. She'd stopped trying to control everything and had started just... participating in her life instead of managing it.

She was sitting in her garden now, watching the sun set and thinking about Jerry. Jerry, who she'd been trying to figure out for months. Jerry, who was complicated and difficult and wonderful and frustrating. Jerry, who she'd been approaching like a problem to be solved instead of a person to be known.

Her phone rang. It **was Jerry.**

"Hey," he said. "I know this is random, but I was just thinking about you. Want to grab dinner? No agenda, no plan, just... dinner."

Margaret looked up at the sky, where the first stars were beginning to appear. Somewhere up there, she had the strangest feeling that someone was smiling.

"Yes," she said. "I'd like that very much."

....

The Angel of Bureaucracy had stopped panicking and started watching. The clipboard had stopped being on fire and had started growing flowers. Small ones, like the kind that grow in sidewalk cracks.

"Sir?" the angel said quietly. "I think I understand now."

God nodded without opening divine eyes. "Tell me."

"It was never about the management, was it? It was about the trust."

"Go on."

"You weren't managing the universe. You were... holding space for it. Believing in it. Trusting it to be what it already was."

"And now?"

The angel looked out at the vast expanse of existence, where quadrillions of beings were going about their lives, making choices, growing, learning, loving, being kind to each other, not because they had to, but because they wanted to.

"Now they're trusting themselves."

God opened one eye and looked at the angel with something that might have been pride. "What does that make you?"

The Angel of Bureaucracy looked down at the clipboard, where the flowers were now blooming into a small garden. The filing systems had reorganized themselves into something that looked suspiciously like art.

"Unemployed," the angel said, and for the first time in its existence, it sounded happy about it.

....

In a small town in Montana, a man named Dale was looking up at the stars and thinking about his father, who had died the previous winter. Dale had been angry about it—angry at the cancer, angry at the doctors, angry at God for letting it happen.

Tonight, though, the anger was gone. Not because the cancer made sense now, or because the doctors had done anything different, or because God had provided some cosmic explanation. The anger was gone because Dale had finally understood that his father's death wasn't a failure of management. It was just what happened. Life and death, joy and sorrow, meeting and parting, all of it part of the same mysterious dance.

Dale's father had lived well. He'd been kind to his family, generous to his neighbors, and patient with fools. He'd taught Dale to fish, to change a tire, to treat people with respect regardless of their station in life. He'd died surrounded by people who loved him, having made the world a little bit better for having been in it.

That was enough. More **than enough.**

Dale looked up at the stars and, for the first time since the funeral, **he smiled.**

"Thanks, Dad," he said to the night sky. "I get **it now.**"

The stars, which had been shining without supervision for billions of years, continued **to shine.**

. . . .

God was dreaming.

This was new. Gods aren't supposed to dream—they're supposed to be constantly aware, perpetually vigilant, always on duty. But in the hammock, suspended between the pillars of crystallized time, God was finally able to let go of the need to know everything all at once.

In the dream, God was a child again, before the weight of infinity had settled on divine shoulders. A child who had just discovered the ability to create, who was making universes like sandcastles, delighting in the simple joy of bringing something into being and then watching it grow beyond what was originally imagined.

In the dream, every being in every world was also a child, playing in the cosmic sandbox, creating their own little universes of meaning and connection and love.

In the dream, no one needed to be managed, because everyone was already whole.

God woke up laughing.

....

The Angel of Bureaucracy was tending its garden now, having discovered that flowers were much more interesting than filing systems. The other angels had stopped by to check on the crisis, but they'd ended up staying to help with the gardening. The Angel of Righteous Wrath had turned out to have a gift for roses. The Angel of Divine Justice was surprisingly good with herbs.

"Sir?" the Angel of Bureaucracy said. "The mortals are asking questions."

"What kind of questions?"

"They want to know if you're okay. They're not asking for anything. They're just... worried about you."

God sat up in the hammock, genuinely surprised. "They're worried about me?"

"A little girl in Bangladesh prayed, 'Dear God, I hope you got enough sleep today.' A man in Iceland said, 'Thanks for everything, and please take care of yourself.' A grandmother in Mexico lit a candle 'for God's happiness.'"

God was quiet for a long moment, feeling something that was entirely new in the catalog of divine emotions.

"They're taking care of me," God said wonderfully.

"Yes, Sir."

"By taking care of each other."

"Yes, Sir."

"By taking care of themselves."

"Yes, Sir."

God lay back down in the hammock and sighed, but this time it was the sigh of someone who had just received the most beautiful gift imaginable.

"It's already done," God whispered again, but this time the words contained a different kind of completion. Not the exhaustion of a job finished, but the satisfaction of a job that had never needed to be done in the first place, because it was already perfect.

....

On Earth, night was falling in some places and day was breaking in others, and everywhere, people were discovering that they were exactly where they needed to be.

In Tokyo, Hiroshi was having dinner with the philosophy professor from the coffee cart, discussing the nature of time over an excellent bowl of ramen.

In São Paulo, Carmen was visiting Eduardo's father in the hospital, having become part of a family she'd never met through the simple act **of caring.**

In Lagos, Adunni was reading to the children who now had new books, and they were reading to her, and somehow they were all learning together.

In Montana, Dale was calling his sister to tell her he loved her, just because he wanted her **to know.**

In Margaret's town, Margaret and Jerry were having diner, not trying to figure each other out, just enjoying each other's company, discovering that love wasn't a problem to be solved, but a gift to be received.

And in a million other places, in a billion other ways, people were being kind to each other for no reason other than that kindness felt like the most natural thing in **the world.**

....

The next morning (though time had become somewhat flexible since the cosmic administrator had clocked out), God woke up naturally, without an alarm, without a to-do list, without the weight of infinity pressing down on divine consciousness.

The hammock swayed gently in a breeze that smelled like jasmine **and possibility.**

The Angel of Bureaucracy was nowhere to be seen, but there was a note pinned to a nearby pillar of crystallized time: "Gone to start a garden in the Crab Nebula. Thank you for teaching me that growth happens better without supervision. —Your Former Assistant (Current Flower Enthusiast)"

God smiled and stretched, and somewhere in the Andromeda Galaxy, a star was born just for the joy **of it.**

The universe was running itself, and it was **running perfectly.**

Not because it was being managed, but because it had finally been trusted to be what it had always been: a **magnificent, chaotic,** beautiful, impossible miracle that worked better when it was allowed **to work.**

God got up from the hammock, not because there was anywhere particular to go, but because it felt good to move. Divine feet touched the ground, and immediately, small flowers began to bloom where they had stepped. Not because God willed it, but because the universe was so happy to have its friend back that it couldn't help but **celebrate**.

And so God walked through existence, not as a manager, administrator, or cosmic boss, but as a participant in the dance, one more being among countless beings, all of them part of the same magnificent, self-organizing, endlessly creative mystery.

It was **already done.**
It had always **been done.**
It would always **be done.**
And that was the most blasphemous, beautiful truth **of all.**

....

Author's Note: This bedtime story is dedicated to everyone who has ever tried to manage the unmanageable, control the uncontrollable, or fix what was never broken in the first place. May you find your own cosmic hammock and discover the radical peace of letting life live itself.

Sweet dreams.

The Already Feast

A Subversive Dinner Party

....

The invitation arrived on paper that felt like velvet between your fingers, written in ink the color of twilight: *You are cordially invited to the Already Feast. No preparation required. You are perfectly dressed. You are perfectly hungry. You are perfectly ready. The table is set.*

....

The address led to a building that seemed to exist in the space between memory and dream—not quite there when you looked directly at it, but solid enough under your feet as you climbed the stairs. The door opened before you could knock, revealing a hallway that smelled of cinnamon and candlewax and something indefinable that reminded you of childhood summers.

The dining room stretched impossibly far in all directions, yet felt intimate as a kitchen table. Golden light spilled from chandeliers made of crystallized laughter, casting warm shadows that moved like slow dancers across walls lined with windows that showed, not the outside world, but glimpses of moments when you had felt totally satisfied: the taste of your grandmother's soup on a sick day, the weight of a sleeping cat in your lap, the feeling of sun on your face during an afternoon nap.

The tables were already set for hundreds of guests, yet somehow there was exactly one perfect seat for each person. Yours was positioned precisely where you needed it to be, as if the room had rearranged itself around your arrival. The chairs were upholstered in fabric that felt like being hugged. The plates were made of some material that looked like moonlight on water, shifting and gleaming as **you moved.**

But strangest of all were the other guests. They sat in their chairs with the particular stillness of people who had **already eaten** everything they needed. Their faces held the soft, dreamy expression of deep satisfaction, the look of someone who has just pushed back from a perfect meal with a contented sigh. Yet the feast was **only beginning.**

An elderly woman with silver hair piled like spun clouds smiled at you across the table. "Welcome," she said, her voice warm as honey. "Isn't it wonderful to finally be full?"

You looked down at yourself, expecting to feel the familiar gnawing of want, the hollow space that usually drove you to seek and strive and reach for more. Instead, you found a curious sensation of completeness, as if you had already eaten something exquisite and forgotten what it was, leaving only the lingering satisfaction.

"But we haven't eaten anything yet," **you said.**

A man with kind eyes and flour dusting his apron appeared beside your chair. He might have been the host, the chef, or another guest who had learned the secret of serving what was already present.

"Ah," he said, setting down a plate that seemed to hold liquid starlight, "but you have. You've been feasting your entire life. Tonight, we simply remember what we've been tasting **all along.**"

First Course: Amuse-Bouche of **Present Moments**

The first dish appeared without fanfare, as if it had always been there: tiny spoons carved from crystallized time, each holding a single drop of something that looked like liquid morning light.

"Amuse-Bouche of Present Moments," the server announced, though whether they were the same person who had greeted you or someone entirely different was impossible to tell. "Distilled from the seconds you forgot to notice. Seasoned with the breath you're breathing right now."

You lifted the spoon, and immediately the dining room filled with the sound of your own heartbeat, not amplified or artificial, but simply noticed for perhaps the first time. The liquid touched your tongue and exploded into flavor: the taste of being alive, of blood moving through veins, of lungs expanding with air that had traveled across oceans to reach you.

It was the flavor of this moment, exactly as it was. Not the moment you were waiting for, not the moment you remembered or anticipated, but the one you were actually living. It tasted like acceptance with undertones of relief and a finish that lingered like the echo of a bell.

Around the table, other guests were closing their eyes, tiny smiles playing at the corners of their mouths. The elderly woman across from you opened her eyes and met **your gaze.**

"I've been trying to taste this for seventy-three years," she said softly. "Funny how it was **always there.**"

The empty spoons dissolved into sparkles of light that settled into your skin like stardust, leaving behind a sensation of being utterly here, completely now, with nowhere else you needed **to be.**

Second Course: Soup of **Unhurried Time**

The bowls materialized slowly, as if time itself were pouring them into existence. They were the deep blue-black of midnight sky, filled with a broth that steamed with the scent of slowness—if slowness had a smell. It would be lavender and rain-washed stones and the particular quiet that settles over the world at three in the morning when everyone else **is asleep.**

"Soup of Unhurried Time," came the announcement, "simmered for exactly as long as it needed. Made from hours you thought you didn't have, garnished with the pauses **between thoughts.**"

You dipped your spoon—a simple silver thing that felt familiar in your hand, like something you'd owned since childhood—and brought the broth to your lips. It was warm in a way that spread through your entire body, loosening muscles you hadn't realized were tense, unknotting urgencies you'd been carrying like rocks in **your pockets.**

The flavor was complex and simple at once: the taste of Sunday afternoons with no plans, of conversations that meandered without destination, of watching clouds change shape without needing them to become anything specific. There were notes of patience aged in caves of contentment, hints of the particular satisfaction that comes from doing one thing at **a time.**

As you swallowed, you felt your internal clock—that relentless timekeeper that usually drummed its fingers impatiently in your chest—begin to slow. Not stop, but breathe. The seconds stretched like taffy, becoming elastic, **generous, sufficient.**

A young man to your left set down his spoon and laughed, not at anything in particular, but with the pure joy of someone who had just remembered that time was not a river rushing past, but an ocean in which he had always been floating.

"I don't think I've been late for anything in my life," he said wonderingly. "I've just been early for things that hadn't happened yet."

The soup bowls emptied slowly, savored rather than consumed, and when they finally vanished, they left behind a sensation of having all the time in the world, which you realized, you always had.

Third Course: Roasted Sunset Gratitude with Caramelized Wonder

The main course arrived like a small sunset on each plate: layers of golden and amber and deep orange that seemed to glow from within. The aroma rose in waves of warmth and richness: the smell of bread baking, of autumn leaves, of moments when you had felt so thankful that the feeling threatened to lift you off **the ground.**

"Roasted Sunset Gratitude," the server explained, "slow-roasted in an oven of appreciation until it falls apart at the touch of a fork. Served with caramelized wonder: those moments when you stopped and really looked at something ordinary and found it absolutely extraordinary."

The first bite was revelation. It tasted like every sunset you'd ever watched, but also like the sunsets you'd missed while rushing somewhere else. The gratitude was sweet and savory at once, with a depth that spoke of years spent learning to notice what was already present. The caramelized wonder provided a counterpoint: bursts of surprise and delight, the flavor of a child seeing snow for the first time, of catching your reflection in a window and thinking, just for a moment, that you looked **exactly right.**

As you chewed, memories bloomed on your tongue: the taste of your mother's singing while she cooked dinner, the feeling of your pet's fur under your hands, the color of light filtering through leaves on a walk you took last Tuesday without really seeing it. Each bite revealed layers of appreciation you'd been accumulating without realizing, small moments of thankfulness that had been seasoning your life all along.

The texture was perfect, tender enough to fall apart, substantial enough to satisfy. It filled spaces in you that you hadn't known were empty, not because you lacked anything, but because you'd forgotten how to taste what you already had.

A woman across the table closed her eyes as she ate, tears of contentment sliding down her cheeks. "It tastes like coming home," she murmured, "to a home I never knew I'd built."

The plates seemed to refill themselves with each bite, offering an endless supply of gratitude and wonder, until finally you realized you couldn't take another mouthful, not because you were overfull, but because you were perfectly satisfied. The sensation was foreign and familiar at once: the feeling of having had exactly enough.

Fourth Course: Poached Clarity in Broth of No Seeking

The next course arrived like a revelation: a single, perfect sphere floating in a bowl of crystal-clear broth that reflected the candlelight like captured stars. The sphere was translucent, shifting between

colors that had no names, pearl and silver and the exact shade
of understanding.

"Poached Clarity," came the gentle announcement, "prepared by
removing everything that was never actually there. Served in a broth
of no seeking made from the moments when you stopped looking for
what you thought you needed and found what was already present."

The broth itself was nearly flavorless, or perhaps it contained
every flavor in perfect balance, canceling each other out until only
essence remained. It was the taste of clean water after a long thirst,
of breathing easily after holding your breath, of the silence between
notes that makes music possible.

When you touched the sphere with your spoon, it dissolved immediately, releasing a burst of pure knowing directly onto your tongue.
Not wisdom or information or understanding in the usual sense, but
the simple, undeniable knowledge that you were exactly where you
belonged, exactly when you belonged there, exactly as you belonged
to be.

It was the flavor of recognition, the taste of remembering something
you'd always known, but had somehow forgotten. Like suddenly
understanding the punchline to a joke you'd been hearing your
whole life, or finding a word you'd been reaching for and realizing it
had been on the tip of your tongue all along.

The clarity didn't make anything clearer in the intellectual sense.
Instead, it dissolved the feeling that anything needed to be clearer.
It was the taste of the moment when seeking stops, not because

you've found what you were looking for, but because you realize you were never **actually lost.**

A teenager at the far end of the table set down his spoon and stared at his hands as if seeing them for the first time. "I don't think I need to become anything," he said quietly, his voice filled with wonder. "I think I already am."

The empty bowls shimmered once and vanished, leaving behind a sensation of profound simplicity; the feeling of being a human being instead of a human doing, of existing rather than becoming, of arriving at a destination you'd never **actually left.**

Fifth Course: Braised Tenderness in Reduction of Self-Compassion

The fifth course appeared like an embrace made edible: tender morsels in a sauce so rich and dark it seemed to contain all the comfort in the world. The aroma was maternal, protective, the smell of being cared for, of being seen and accepted exactly as you were, mess **and all.**

"Braised Tenderness in Reduction of Self-Compassion," the server said, their voice soft as a lullaby. "Slow-cooked until it releases its defenses. The reduction is made from forgiveness that's been simmering for years, concentrated into pure kindness."

The first bite was like being held. The tenderness fell apart in your mouth, releasing flavors of acceptance and understanding. The sauce was complex: notes of patience, hints of love that doesn't need you to be different, undertones of the relief that comes when you finally stop fighting yourself.

It tasted like every time someone had said "it's okay" and **meant it.** Like the moment when self-criticism finally runs out of things **to say.** Like the warmth that spreads through your chest when you catch yourself being human and choose to find it endearing rather **than disappointing.**

As you ate, you felt your internal critic, that voice that usually provided running commentary on your every move, grow quieter. Not silenced, but softer, as if it had finally been fed something nourishing enough to satisfy its hunger **for perfection.**

The texture was impossibly comforting, like being wrapped in the softest blanket while rain patters against the windows. Each bite seemed to heal some small wound you'd been carrying, not through dramatic revelation, but through the simple act of being gentle with yourself.

A middle-aged man to your right began to laugh, not at anything humorous, but with the pure joy of someone who had just realized he didn't have to be his own worst enemy. "I've been so mean to myself," he said, still chuckling. "For no reason at all. What a funny thing to do."

The plates emptied slowly, lovingly, and when they disappeared, they left behind a sensation of being your own best friend: patient, kind, and endlessly forgiving.

Sixth Course: Seared Spontaneity with Essence of Unscripted Joy

The sixth course burst onto the table like laughter made solid: plates that seemed to dance and shift, colors that had no business existing in food, but somehow did: electric blues and singing purples the exact shade of a child's giggle.

"Seared Spontaneity with Essence of Unscripted Joy," came the announcement, though the server's voice was barely audible over the sound of the dishes themselves: a gentle humming, like the vibration of contentment.

The searing had created a crust of pure surprise on each morsel, crackling with the energy of moments when plans dissolve and something better takes their place. Underneath, the spontaneity was tender and yielding, flavored with the particular sweetness of letting go of control and discovering that the universe has been improvising something beautiful all along.

The essence of unscripted joy was scattered around each plate like edible confetti: tiny bursts of flavor that exploded on the tongue with the taste of unexpected phone calls from old friends, of finding money in jacket pockets, of dancing badly in the kitchen while dinner cooks.

Each bite was different from the last, as if the dish was reinventing itself with every forkful. Sometimes it tasted like snow days and cancelled meetings. Sometimes like the moment when a song you'd forgotten comes on the radio and you sing along badly yet perfectly.

Sometimes like the particular joy of being completely, unselfconsciously yourself.

The flavors refused to be analyzed or categorized. They were wild, unplanned, perfectly imperfect. Eating became an act of play rather than consumption, each bite a small celebration of the fact that the best moments in life are usually the ones that were never scheduled.

A young woman across the table began to move her shoulders in time with the humming plates, her face lit with the expression of someone who had just remembered that joy doesn't have to be earned or planned or deserved—it can simply be allowed.

"I used to think happiness was a destination," she said, taking another bite. "But it tastes more like a dance. And I already know all the steps."

The plates continued their gentle humming until the last bite was taken, then dissolved into sparkles of pure delight that settled into the air like a blessing, leaving behind the understanding that joy is not something to achieve but something to notice, and it's always already there.

Seventh Course: Aged Acceptance with Notes of Settled Peace

The penultimate course arrived with the dignity of deep roots and ancient trees: something that looked simple, but revealed its complexity slowly, like wisdom earned through years of being exactly what it was without apology.

"Aged Acceptance with Notes of Settled Peace," the server announced with reverence. "Aged for precisely as long as it took to ripen. Some of the ingredients have been developing since childhood. Others since before you were born."

The appearance was humble: earth tones and gentle curves, nothing flashy or demanding attention. But the aroma was profound.
The smell of oak trees and river stones, of grandmothers' hands and Sunday mornings, of the particular peace that comes from no longer needing to be anywhere other than where you are.

The first taste was like coming home to yourself. The acceptance was full-bodied and complex, with layers of making peace with your own contradictions, of embracing your own particular way of being human, of finally understanding that you were never meant to be anyone other than exactly who you are.

The notes of settled peace provided a foundation, the flavor of no longer fighting reality, of letting the river of life carry you instead of swimming upstream, of the profound relief that comes when you stop trying to be the author of everything and consent to be the protagonist of your own ordinary, extraordinary story.

It was aged to perfection, not the harsh edges of fresh ambition or the bitterness of unripe comparison, but the mellow richness of time that has taught you the difference between what you can change and what you can accept, and the wisdom to know which is which.

As you ate, you felt your shoulders drop in a way they hadn't in years. The constant, low-level tension of trying to be someone else, somewhere else, something else finally released its grip. You were here. You were this. You **were enough.**

An elderly gentleman at the head of the table closed his eyes and smiled with deep satisfaction. "I spent so many years trying to improve myself," he said softly. "What a relief to discover I was already cooked through."

The course lingered longer than the others, as if it understood its own importance. When it finally faded, it left behind a sensation of being perfectly settled in your own skin, like a cat finding the right spot in a patch of sunlight and knowing this is where it belongs.

Final Course: Essence of **Already Complete**

The final course was almost not there at all, just the faintest shimmer on each plate, like heat waves rising from summer pavement or the gleam of light on water that appears and disappears with each breath.

"Essence of Already Complete," came the whispered announcement. "The most difficult dish to prepare, because it requires removing everything that was added to something that was perfect from **the beginning.**"

You lifted your fork, though it seemed practically unnecessary. The essence was barely substantial enough to taste, yet it filled your mouth with the flavor of wholeness, not the wholeness you achieve through effort or accumulation, but the wholeness you discover when you finally stop trying to add pieces to something that was never broken.

It tasted like the moment you realize you've been carrying keys to a door that isn't locked. Like finding out that the treasure you've been seeking was buried in your own backyard all along. Like understanding that every journey is really a journey home to something you never actually left.

The flavor was familiar yet startling: the taste of your own breath, of your own heartbeat, of the simple fact of your existence before you learned to have opinions about it. It was the flavor of being enough before you learned to want more, of being perfect before you learned about improvement, of being complete before you learned about incompleteness.

As the essence dissolved on your tongue, you felt every hunger you'd ever known—for success, for love, for understanding, for validation, for meaning—reveal itself as the same hunger. The hunger to return to something you'd never actually lost. The hunger to become something you'd always already been.

Around the table, every guest was still. Not the stillness of waiting or wanting, but the stillness of arrival. The stillness of recognizing that the feast you'd been seeking your entire life was the one you'd been eating all along, bite by unconscious bite, moment by unnoticed moment.

The plates shimmered once more and vanished, leaving nothing behind except the most startling realization of all: that you were not less full than when you'd arrived. You were exactly as satisfied as you'd always been. You had simply, finally, remembered how to taste it.

After the Feast

The dining room began to fade around the edges, like watercolors bleeding into white paper. The other guests rose from their seats with the particular grace of people who had nowhere urgent to be, nothing pressing to accomplish, no need to digest what they'd just experienced, because they'd been living it all along.

The elderly woman with silver hair paused beside your chair. "Funny," she said, her eyes twinkling, "how the most satisfying meal is the one where you realize you were never **actually hungry.**"

One by one, the guests made their way toward doors that appeared wherever they needed them to be. The doors led not to the outside world, but to the inside world, to the ordinary Tuesday morning and grocery store afternoon and tired Thursday evening of their regular lives. But they carried with them the knowledge that every moment was already seasoned with enough, already prepared and complete, served at the table of their own existence.

You remained in your chair for a moment longer, tasting the lingering flavors of acceptance, clarity, and unhurried time. The sensations in your body were of deep satisfaction, not the heaviness of overindulgence, but the perfect fullness of someone who had eaten exactly what they needed, when they needed it, in precisely the **right amount.**

When you finally stood, your legs were steady, your breath was easy, and your heart felt the particular lightness that comes not from emptiness, but from the absence of artificial weight. You had arrived at the feast carrying invisible burdens: the hunger for **more, the** anxiety of not enough, the constant subtle dissatisfaction that flavors so much of **ordinary life.**

You were leaving with empty hands and a full heart, carrying nothing except the knowledge that every meal you'd ever eaten had been a course in this feast. Every moment of satisfaction, every pause of contentment, every instant when you'd felt perfectly aligned with exactly what was happening, all of it had been training your palate for the radical flavor **of enough.**

The door appeared exactly where you expected it to be, leading back to your ordinary life. But as you reached for the handle, you understood that you weren't returning to the same world you'd left. You were returning to the same world you'd always lived in, but with taste buds finally calibrated to detect the feast that had been happening all along.

The invitation was still in your pocket, though the paper now felt ordinary, just paper, after all. But written on the back, in hand-writing that looked suspiciously like your own, were the words: *Every meal is the Already Feast. Every moment is already seasoned with enough. Bon appétit.*

You stepped through the door and back into your life, carrying with you the lingering taste of being perfectly, completely, finally satisfied, not because you had consumed something special, but because you had finally learned to taste what you'd been eating all along.

The feast **was over.**
The feast was **just beginning.**
The feast had **never stopped.**

....

Author's Note: This subversive dinner party is an invitation to taste your own life differently. The dishes served at the Already Feast exist in every ordinary meal, every quiet moment, every breath taken without thinking about it. The sensory memory of this fictional feast may linger longer than expected, a somatic reminder that satisfaction is not a destination, but a way of tasting what's already on your plate.

Enjoy.

The Silent Permission Slip

A Participatory Fable

The library had been abandoned for seventeen years.

Maya discovered this from the brass plaque by the door, green
with age and obscured by ivy that seemed to grow in deliberate
spirals. The building itself crouched between two glass towers like
a forgotten thought, its red brick facade weathered to the color of
dried blood, its windows dark as closed eyes.

She hadn't meant to find it. She'd been walking aimlessly through
the city, trying to outpace the conversation that kept looping in her
head—her manager's voice, sharp with disappointment: *"Maya, I need
to see more initiative. More innovation. More... more."* Always more.
Never enough.

The brass handle turned easily under her hand, as if it had been waiting.

Inside, dust motes danced in shafts of amber light that slanted through tall windows. The air smelled of old paper and something else—something like the moment before rain, when the atmosphere holds its breath. Shelves stretched toward a vaulted ceiling, heavy with books that no one had touched in nearly **two decades.**

Maya's footsteps echoed in the silence, each sound swallowed quickly by the weight of accumulated quiet. She moved without purpose through the stacks, her fingers trailing along leather spines, reading titles in languages she didn't recognize, in scripts that seemed to shift when she wasn't looking directly **at them.**

Reference. Philosophy. Forgotten Sciences.
Cartography of Unmapped Territories.

She found herself in a section labeled simply "Permissions" in faded **gold lettering.**

The books here were different. Thinner. Some were no thicker than pamphlets, their covers plain and worn smooth by countless hands. Maya pulled one from the shelf at random: *On the Art of Arriving Without Traveling.* Another: *Licenses for the Unlicensed.* A third: *The Bureaucracy of the Heart: Forms to File **with Yourself.***

At the end of the row, in a space that seemed designed for exactly one book, she found a volume bound in green cloth, its spine unmarked.

When she opened it, all the pages were blank except for the first, which contained a single sentence in **elegant script**:

*The most important permissions are the ones we **give ourselves.***

Maya stared at the words until they seemed to pulse with their own rhythm. She turned the page, expecting more text, but found only clean white paper. Page after page of it, as if the book was waiting for something to be written.

She was about to close it when she noticed the small envelope tucked into the **back cover.**

The envelope was cream-colored, expensive-looking, with her name written on it in the same elegant script. Not "Maya" or "M. Chen" or any of the variations she was used to seeing, but her full name: *Maya Lin Chen*, written as if the person who had penned it knew exactly who she was and had been **expecting her.**

Her hands trembled slightly as she **opened it.**

Inside was a single slip of paper, blank and slightly rough to the touch, like expensive stationery. No message. No instructions. Just the paper itself, waiting.

Maya looked around the empty library, half-expecting to see someone watching her, but she was alone with the dust and the books and the strange, expectant silence.

She folded the paper carefully and slipped it into her **jacket pocket.**

．．

That night, Maya dreamed of signatures.

She was sitting at an enormous desk in a room with **no walls,**
signing document after document. Permission slips for her childhood
self to cry when she was hurt. Release forms for her teenage self
to fail without shame. Waivers for her adult self to love imperfectly,
to make mistakes, to not know what she was doing half **the time.**

Each signature felt like letting go of something she'd been carrying
without realizing **its weight.**

She woke with the taste of ink on her tongue and the strange
certainty that the blank slip of paper in her jacket pocket had grown
heavier overnight.

．．

The next few days passed in a blur of meetings and deadlines, but
Maya found herself reaching for the paper constantly. In the elevator,
waiting for the doors to close. During presentations, when her boss's
eyes swept the room like searchlights. In the bathroom stall, stealing
moments of privacy between the demands of a day that never seemed
to end.

She never took it out, just touched it through the fabric of her
pocket, feeling its edges, its weight, its strange warmth.

On Thursday, her colleague James stopped by her desk with coffee and the tired smile of someone who'd also spent the week trying to transform himself into more than he was.

"You seem different," he said, settling into the chair across from her. "Calmer, maybe?"

Maya paused in her typing. Was she calmer? She thought about the conversation with her boss on Monday, how it had sent her spiraling into the familiar vortex of self-criticism and desperate strategizing. But today, when he'd made another comment about "stepping up" and "rising to the challenge," she'd simply nodded and kept working.

Not because she didn't care, but because somewhere deep inside, a small voice had whispered: *What if you're **already enough**?*

"Maybe," she said. "I found something interesting the **other day.**"

"Oh yeah? What kind **of interesting?**"

Maya's hand moved to her pocket, touched the paper. "A library. An old one. Full of books **about... permissions.**"

James raised an eyebrow. "Permissions **for what?**"

"That's the thing," Maya said slowly. "I think we're supposed to figure that out ourselves."

That weekend, Maya returned to **the library.**

The door opened as easily as before, the brass handle warm under her palm despite the October chill. Inside, the light seemed different—softer, more golden, as if the building itself had been waiting for her return.

She made her way back to the Permissions section and pulled the green book from its place on the shelf. This time, when she opened it, she found more than just the single sentence. New words had appeared, as if written by an invisible hand:

*Permissions are not granted. They are claimed. They are **not earned**. They are taken. They are not deserved. They are **simply... allowed**.*

The slip of paper you carry contains no magic except the magic you give it. No power except the power you choose to invest in it. No meaning except the meaning you decide it holds.

*What do you need **permission for**?*

The question hung in the air like incense, filling the space around her with its weight. Maya sank into a nearby reading chair, the green book open in her lap, **and considered.**

What did she need **permission for**?

The answers came slowly at first, then faster, like water through a crack in **a dam:**

Permission to be ordinary. To have a job instead of a calling. To earn enough money without it defining her worth. To spend Sundays reading instead of networking. To say no without explaining why. To disappoint people sometimes. To disappoint **herself somtimes.** To not optimize every single moment for **productivity, growth, or improvement.**

Permission to be sad when she was sad, without immediately trying to fix it or find the lesson or transform it into motivation. Permission to be happy when she was happy, without waiting for the other shoe to drop or feeling guilty about others who **were suffering.**

Permission to not know what she wanted from life beyond the simple desire to wake up each morning without dread. Permission to be enough, exactly as she was, without addition or subtraction or endless renovation.

The list could have gone on forever. Maya realized she'd been carrying around a catalog of things she thought she needed approval for, as if there were some cosmic authority figure whose job it was to grant her the right to exist in her own skin.

She pulled the slip of paper from her pocket and smoothed it on the table beside the book.

It looked impossibly small and ordinary in the golden light—just a piece of cream-colored paper, blank and waiting. But as she stared at it, Maya began to understand what the library was asking **of her.**

Not to read more books about permission. Not to study the theory of self-acceptance or memorize affirmations **about worthiness.**

Just to write it down. To make it real in the only way that mattered: in her own handwriting, in her own words, in her own time.

Maya looked around the library for a pen and found one tucked between the pages of a book titled *The Art of Self-Authorization.* It was an old fountain pen, heavy and warm, as if it had just been held.

She uncapped it and held it over **the paper.**

*What do you need **permission for?***

Her hand moved almost without her **conscious direction:**

*I give myself permission to **be imperfect.***

The words looked strange in her handwriting, like a language she was still learning to speak. She stared at them for a long moment, then continued:

*I give myself permission to not have all **the answers.***

*I give myself permission to rest without **earning it.***

*I give myself permission to want **simple things.***

*I give myself permission to stop trying to become **someone else.***

Each sentence felt like unlocking a door she hadn't realized was closed. Maya's handwriting, usually cramped and hurried, began to flow across the paper with increasing confidence:

*I give myself permission to be enough, exactly as I am, right now, without changing a **single thing**.*

*I give myself permission to quit the job of being my own **worst critic.***

*I give myself permission to **like myself.***

*I give myself permission to forgive myself for not **being perfect.***

*I give myself permission to take up exactly the amount of space I **take up.***

*I give myself permission to matter without having to **prove it.***

*I give myself permission to exist **without justification.***

Maya's hand was shaking by the time she reached the bottom of the paper. Not from fear, but from something that felt like relief so profound it bordered on grief. As if she were mourning all the years she'd spent asking for permissions that she'd always had the authority to grant herself.

She set the pen down and looked at what she'd written. The words seemed to glow in the afternoon light, not with any mystical energy, but with the simple power of **truth acknowledged.**

For several minutes, Maya sat in the quiet of the library, the slip of paper in front of her, feeling something fundamental shift in her chest. Not a dramatic transformation—no lightning bolts or sudden enlightenment—just a quiet settling, like a house finding its foundation after years of shifting.

Then, without quite knowing why, she tore the paper into small pieces.

The sound was surprisingly loud in the library's silence. Maya held the fragments in her cupped palms, looking at her own words now broken into syllables and letters, scattered and rearranged into new, meaningless patterns.

She stood and walked to one of the tall windows. It opened easily, letting in a breeze that smelled of autumn leaves and the promise of rain. Maya held her hands out the window and **opened them.**

The pieces of paper caught the wind immediately, spinning and dancing in the air before disappearing around the corner of the building, carried away to places she would never know.

Maya watched until the last fragment vanished, then closed the window and turned back to the library.

The green book **was gone.**

She looked on the table where she'd left it, then in the chair, then on the shelves. But it was nowhere to be found, as if it had dissolved the moment she no longer **needed it.**

Maya smiled. She understood now that the magic had never been in the book or the paper or even the library itself. The magic had been in the act of writing her own permissions, in the radical idea that she didn't need anyone else's approval to give herself what she'd been seeking all along.

She walked back through the stacks, past the books on unmapped territories and forgotten sciences, past the philosophy section, and the reference desk. At the front door, she paused and looked back one more time.

The library seemed smaller somehow, more ordinary. Just an old building full of old books, no more mysterious than any other abandoned place. But Maya knew that it would be here if she ever needed it again, or if someone else needed to find a blank slip of paper and remember that the most important permissions are the ones we give ourselves.

She stepped out into the afternoon light and began walking home, her pockets empty but her shoulders somehow lighter than they'd been in years.

....

The next Monday, Maya's boss called her into his office.

"Maya," he said, settling behind his desk with **the particular** expression he wore when he was about to deliver one of his speeches about exceeding expectations and maximizing potential. "I've been thinking about our conversation last week. About stepping up, taking **more initiative.**"

Maya nodded, feeling the familiar tightness begin to form in her chest. Then she remembered the slip of paper, the words she'd written in her own hand, the feeling of watching them disappear on the wind. The tightness didn't disappear entirely, but it loosened, like a fist slowly opening.

"I want you to know," her boss continued, "that I appreciate the work you've been doing. But I think you have so much more potential that you're not tapping into. I'd like to see you really push yourself, you know? Challenge yourself to be more than you think you can be."

Maya looked at him across the desk, this man who meant well, but who had somehow appointed himself the manager of her potential, the supervisor of her self-worth. A month ago, this conversation would have sent her into a spiral of analysis and self-improvement planning. She would have gone home and made lists of ways to be better, more impressive, more worthy of his approval.

Instead, she heard herself say, calmly, "I think I'm doing good work."

Her boss blinked, clearly not expecting this response. "Well, yes, of course. But don't you want to excel? Don't you want to really make **your mark?**"

Maya considered this. Did she want to excel? Did she want to make her mark? The questions felt strange now, like being asked if she wanted to become someone she'd never met.

"I want to do work that matters to me," she said finally. "I want to do it well. I want to go home at the end of the day feeling like I contributed something useful. I think **that's enough.**"

The word hung in the air between **them:** *enough.*

Her boss shifted uncomfortably. "But Maya, you're capable of so much more."

"Maybe," Maya said. "But more isn't always better. Sometimes, more is just more."

She could see him struggling with this concept, this idea that someone might voluntarily choose adequacy over ambition, competence over conquest. It was a foreign language to him, this vocabulary **of sufficiency.**

"Well," he said finally, "I just hope you don't come to regret not pushing yourself harder."

Maya smiled. "I think I'll regret a lot of things in my life," she said. "But being content isn't going to be one of them."

....

That evening, Maya met James for dinner. He was full of his usual anxieties about performance reviews and promotion timelines, the elaborate chess game he was playing with his own career.

"I just feel like I'm not doing enough," he said, stabbing at his salad with unnecessary force. "Like everyone else has figured out some secret to success that I'm missing. Do you ever feel **that way?**"

Maya thought about the question while she chewed her pasta. A month ago, she would have said yes immediately, would have launched into her own catalog of inadequacies and missed opportunities. Now, though, she found the question **itself puzzling.**

"What if there's no secret?" she said. "What if everyone else is just making it up as they go along, the same **as us?**"

James looked at her skeptically. "Come on, Maya. Some people definitely have their **lives together.**"

"Do they, though? Or do they just look like they do from **the outside?**"

"I mean, look at Sarah from accounting. Promoted twice in three years, always has these amazing weekend plans, seems to have everything **figured out.**"

Maya smiled. "Sarah from accounting told me last week that she cries in her car after work, because she's so overwhelmed. Those amazing weekend plans? She schedules them, because she's terrified of having unstructured time to think about whether she's **actually happy.**"

James stared at her. "She told **you that?**"

"She did. People tell you things when you stop pretending you have everything figured out. When you stop competing with them for who can seem the most successful."

"So what, we just... give up? **Stop trying?**"

Maya twirled pasta around her fork, thinking. "Not give up. Just... give ourselves permission to be human. To be imperfect. To not have to constantly prove our worth **through achievement.**"

She could see James wrestling with this idea, the same way she had wrestled with it herself. The same way her boss had wrestled with it that morning. There was something almost heretical about suggesting that you could just... be enough. That you could choose to step off the hamster wheel of constant self-improvement and just exist in your own skin without apology.

"Where is this coming from?" James asked. "This... zen thing you've got going on?"

Maya laughed. "I found a library," she said. "And in that library, I found a book. And in that book, I found a piece of paper. And on that paper, I wrote myself a permission slip."

"A permission slip **for what?**"

"To stop trying to become **someone else.**"

James was quiet for a long moment, considering this. "Did **it work?**"

Maya looked around the restaurant, at all the people eating and talking and living their ordinary lives. A few months ago, she would have been studying them, trying to figure out what they knew that she didn't, how they'd achieved whatever level of contentment or success she imagined they possessed.

Now she just saw them as fellow humans, all of them trying to figure it out, all of them probably carrying their own invisible burdens and secret fears. All of them enough, exactly as they were, whether they knew it or not.

"Yeah," she said to James. "I think it did."

....

Six months later, Maya found herself back at **the library.**

Not because she was seeking anything in particular, but because she'd been walking through the city on a Saturday afternoon and her feet had carried her there, the way feet sometimes do when the conscious mind isn't paying attention.

The building looked exactly the same: red brick weathered to the color of dried blood, windows dark as closed eyes, ivy growing in deliberate spirals around the brass plaque by the door.

The handle turned as easily **as ever.**

Inside, the light still slanted through tall windows in golden shafts, dust motes still danced in the air, books still lined the shelves in their patient rows. But something was different. The library felt... lived in. Not abandoned, but **actively waiting.**

Maya made her way to the Permissions section and found several people there, all of them reading quietly, all of them holding small slips of **cream-colored paper.**

A woman with silver hair was writing something with slow, deliberate strokes. A young man was staring at a blank slip, his pen hovering over the paper as if he were afraid to make the first mark. A teenager was folding her completed slip into an origami crane.

Maya smiled and continued walking through the stacks, not wanting to disturb their processes. In the back corner of the library, she found a new section she hadn't noticed before: *Post-Permission Literature.*

The books here had titles like *The Art of Enough, Ordinary Magic,* and *A Field Guide to Being Human.* Maya pulled one at random: *Letters to My Former Self: What I Wish I'd Known* **About Worthiness.**

She opened it and found it filled with handwritten letters, each one different, each one signed with a name she didn't recognize. As she read, she realized that these were letters from people who had found their way to the library, written their own permission slips, and discovered something worth sharing with others who might be walking the same path.

Dear Overachieving Me, one letter began. *You are enough. I know you don't believe this yet. I know you think you need to earn the right to take up space in the world. But I'm writing to tell you that you were born deserving. You were born enough. Everything you're trying so hard to become, you already are.*

Another: *Dear Anxious Me, The thing you're afraid of, being ordinary, isn't actually terrible. Ordinary is where most of life happens. Ordinary is where contentment lives. Ordinary* **is enough.**

And another: *Dear Striving Me, Rest isn't earned. Joy isn't a reward for good behavior. Love isn't a prize for being perfect. These things are your birthright, and you can claim them anytime.*

Maya read letter after letter, each one a small permission slip written by someone who had learned to give themselves what they'd been seeking from the world. She thought about adding her own letter, but realized she didn't need to. The letter she'd written six months ago, the one she'd torn up and let the wind carry away, was still doing its work, still giving her permission to be exactly who she was.

Instead, she pulled out her phone and wrote a text **to James:** *Want to grab dinner tonight? No agenda, no plan, just dinner. And maybe I'll tell you about* **permission slips.**

His response came quickly: *Yes. And maybe I'll ask you where to find some* **good paper.**

Maya smiled and made her way back through the library, past the people in the Permissions section who were still writing their own authorizations to be human, past the shelves full of forgotten sciences and unmapped territories, past the reference desk where someone had left a small sign: *The most important reference is the one you give yourself.*

At the front door, she paused and looked back one more time. The library would be here when people needed it, she knew. It would always be here, in some form or another, because the need to give ourselves permission to be enough was as constant as breathing, as necessary **as water.**

Maya stepped out into the afternoon light, her pockets empty but her heart full, and began walking home through a city full of people who were all, whether they knew it or not, carrying their own invisible permission slips, their own quiet authorizations to take up exactly the amount of space they took up, to matter without having to prove it, to be enough exactly as they were.

The wind picked up, carrying the scent of spring and the promise of rain, and somewhere in the city, small pieces of cream-colored paper danced through the air, carrying permissions that had already been granted, freedoms that had already been claimed, worth that had never needed to be earned in the first place.

....

Now, dear reader, you have reached the end of this fable, but perhaps the beginning of something else.

*Somewhere in your home, you have a piece of paper. Any paper will do: notebook paper, a napkin, the back of an envelope, a receipt you'll never need. It's blank, or **blank enough.***

Somewhere in your home, you have something to write with: a pen, pencil, crayon, marker. It doesn't matter what, only that it **makes marks.**

What do you need **permission for?**

What have you been waiting for someone else to tell you **is okay?**

What would you write on your own **permission slip?**

The paper is waiting. Your handwriting is the only signature that matters. And when you're done—if you choose to be done—you can keep it, or tear it up, or burn it, or let the wind **take it.**

The choice is yours. The permission is yours. It always was.

....

Author's Note: This fable is an invitation disguised as a story. The library exists wherever you choose to find it. The permission slip is as real as you make it. The only magic is the magic you grant yourself: the radical act of writing down, in your own hand, the permissions you've been seeking from the world.

*This page was intentionally left **blank. Hint.***

The Dictionary of Missing Words

A Cognitive Hack

....

*Found in the basement of the Abandoned Library of Almost-Things, written
in margins and between the lines of conventional dictionaries by readers
who discovered that some experiences lived in the spaces between existing
words. Each entry represents a felt sense that had been waiting, sometimes
for decades, to be named.*

....

Abeya
[ah-BAY-ah] noun

The particular relief that floods through your body when you
finally stop trying to make someone understand you. Not the bitter

resignation of giving up, but the sweet release of a burden you didn't realize you were carrying. Often accompanied by a sudden lightness in your chest and an urge for self-kindness.

*Etymology: From the Japanese "akirameru" (to **accept**) + "bayah" (an invented sound **of exhaling**)*

*Example: "After three hours of explaining why the project mattered to her, Maya felt the gentle abeya wash over her as she realized her boss would never truly get it—and that this was **perfectly fine.**"*

Belmost
[BEL-most] adjective

The state of being almost ready to let go of something, but not quite. It's like standing at the edge of a diving board, toes curled over the edge, knowing you will jump, but not yet willing to release your grip on the familiar fear. Contains within it both the tension of holding on and the anticipation of freedom.

Etymology: From "belly" (the physical center where we hold things) + "almost"

*Example: "James felt belmost about his anger toward his father. He could sense the forgiveness waiting just beyond his current understanding, but his fingers weren't quite ready to uncurl from **the grievance.**"*

Candess

[CAN-dess] noun

The moment when you realize you've been performing a version of yourself that you don't actually like, and you suddenly don't have the energy to keep up the charade. Often occurs in bathrooms at parties, cars after meetings, or kitchens late at night. Feels like removing shoes that were always too tight.

Etymology: From "candid" + "undress"

*Example: "Standing in her pristine apartment after another networking event, Sophie experienced a profound candess. The exhaustion of being 'on' finally outweighing her fear of **being ordinary**."*

Dolmering

[DOLL-mer-ing] verb

The act of discovering comfort in your own company after years of believing you were supposed to want more social interaction. Not loneliness transformed into solitude, but the recognition that you were never actually lonely. You were just taught to call your contentment isolation.

Etymology: From "dolmen" (ancient stone structures that stand alone) + "murmuring"

*Example: "After canceling her third social obligation that week, Rebecca realized she wasn't avoiding people; she was dolmering, finally learning to hear the sound of her **own contentment**."*

Ephemind
[EF-eh-mind] noun

The fleeting, but vivid memory of who you were before you learned to worry about who you should become. Usually surfaces unexpectedly: while washing dishes, walking without destination, or in the three seconds after waking, before your identity **reassembles itself.**

Etymology: From "ephemeral" + "remind"

Example: "During his morning shower, David caught an ephemind of his seven-year-old self building elaborate cities in the sandbox, completely absorbed and needing nothing from the world except time and dirt."

Frillow
[FRILL-oh] verb

To allow yourself to enjoy something simple without immediately trying to optimize it, analyze it, or turn it into a habit The act of eating strawberries without researching their nutritional content, of reading poetry without seeking deeper meaning, of lying in grass without setting a timer.

*Etymology: From "frolic" + "pillow" (something soft to **rest in**)*

*Example: "Instead of photographing the sunset for social **media, Elena** decided to frillow the moment, letting the colors wash over her without needing to capture or share **the experience.**"*

Glimph

[GLIMPH] noun

The recognition that a problem you've been wrestling with for months or years has quietly solved itself while you weren't paying attention. Often accompanied by the slightly disorienting feeling of reaching for emotional baggage that's no longer there.

*Etymology: From "onomatopoeia" (the sound of **something dissolving**)*

Example: "Marcus experienced a sudden glimph when he realized he hadn't thought about his ex-girlfriend in weeks, despite spending the previous year convinced he'd never get over her."

Hendreaming

[HEN-dree-ming] verb

The practice of having small, achievable fantasies instead of grand ones. Dreaming of sleeping in on Tuesday rather than winning the lottery. Imagining a really good sandwich rather than a perfect life. The gentle art of wanting things that are actually possible.

*Etymology: From "hen" (domestic, **grounded**) + "dreaming"*

*Example: "While her friends planned elaborate vacation fantasies, Patricia found herself hendreaming about an afternoon with no emails and a book she'd been meaning **to read.**"*

Innerwhelm
[IN-ner-whelm] noun

The opposite of overwhelm: the calm, spacious feeling of having enough energy for whatever is actually in front of you, as opposed to everything you're imagining might be in front of you. Often occurs when you stop preparing for disasters that exist only in your mind.

*Etymology: From "inner" + "whelm" (to engulf, but in a **supportive way**)*

Example: "After years of anxiety, Tom discovered innerwhelm on a random Thursday when he realized he only needed to live through today, not all the potential todays his mind had been rehearsing."

Jelling
[JELL-ing] verb

The process of your scattered pieces coming together, not through effort, but through rest. Like how jello sets when left alone, not when stirred constantly. The patient practice of letting your life organize itself while you're doing other things.

Etymology: From "jell" + "dwelling"

*Example: "After months of forcing career decisions, Amanda started jelling, trusting that clarity would emerge if she stopped trying to **manufacture it**."*

Kenopsia

[ken-OP-see-ah] noun

The peace that settles over you when you realize that your worth isn't determined by how much you achieve, produce, or accomplish. Like finding yourself alone in a space that's usually crowded and discovering you prefer the emptiness.

Etymology: From Greek "kenos" (empty) + "opsis" (sight): seeing the beauty in emptiness

Example: "During her sabbatical, Claire experienced deep kenopsia, understanding for the first time that her value wasn't conditional on her productivity."

Loftitude

[LOFT-ih-tood] noun

The altitude of perspective that allows you to see your problems as weather patterns rather than permanent features of the landscape. The emotional equivalent of climbing high enough that you can see the storm has edges.

Etymology: From "loft" + "altitude"

Example: "From her newfound loftitude, Sarah could see that her family drama was just a squall line that would eventually pass, rather than the permanent climate she'd imagined."

Mellit

[MEL-it] verb

To soften toward yourself in the way honey melts in **warm tea:** gradually, sweetly, without force. The gentle dissolving **of self-**criticism into something **more nourishing.**

Etymology: From Latin "mel" (honey) + "permit"

Example: "As she watched her toddler struggle with shoelaces, Monica began to mellit toward her own imperfections, remembering that learning anything takes time and patience."

Nowness

[NOW-ness] noun

The texture of being completely present without trying to be present. Distinguished from mindfulness by its effortlessness, like suddenly noticing you've been breathing perfectly well without instruction. The natural state that emerges when you stop managing your experience.

Etymology: From "now" + "-ness" (quality of being)

Example: "While waiting for his delayed train, instead of checking his phone, Robert slipped into nowness, simply existing in the station without needing the moment to be different."

Offluence
[OFF-loo-ence] noun

The relief of finally telling someone about a problem you've been carrying alone, not because you want them to fix it, but because secrets grow heavy in isolation. Often followed by the surprising discovery that the problem was smaller than your worry about **the problem.**

Etymology: From "off" + "effluence" (flowing out), a gentle flow of emotional release

Example: "After months of sleepless nights, Jennifer felt a wave of offluence after sharing her financial fears with her sister. The anxiety, once mountainous, melted like a glacier into a tiny puddle."

Plenish
[PLEN-ish] verb

To feel full without having consumed anything. The sensation of satisfaction that comes from appreciating what's already present rather than acquiring what's absent. Often occurs during mundane moments like folding laundry or stirring soup.

*Etymology: From "replenish" without the "re"—being filled for the first time rather **than again***

*Example: "Sitting in her garden with morning coffee, watching bees visit flowers, Pamela found herself plenishing, completely satisfied without needing to add anything to **the moment.**"*

Quietude

[KWHY-eh-tood] noun

The particular silence that exists between thoughts, not empty, but full of potential. Different from meditation or mindfulness, more like the pause between musical notes that makes the melody possible. The space where insights grow.

Etymology: From "quiet" + "attitude"

Example: "In the quietude between her worry about the presentation and her worry about dinner, Lisa found the answer to a problem she'd been struggling with for weeks."

Rightwhere

[RITE-wair] adverb

The feeling of being exactly where you belong, even if where you are isn't where you planned to be. Often occurs in moments of supposed failure, delay, or detour. The deep knowing that every step has brought you precisely to here.

Etymology: From "right" + "where," being in the correct location despite contradictory outward appearances

Example: "Stranded at the airport for six hours, missing his connection and his important meeting, David surprisingly found himself feeling rightwhere, as if this delay was exactly what his overscheduled life needed."

Sofyce

[SOH-fyse] verb

To be enough without addition, modification, or improvement. Not settling or giving up, but recognizing completeness. The verb form of arriving at a destination you didn't know you were **traveling toward.**

*Etymology: From "soft" + Latin "sufficere" (to be adequate), reclaimed from its association with "barely enough" to mean **"perfectly adequate"***

Example: "After years of self-improvement projects, Miguel realized he could simply sofyce; he was already the person he'd been trying to become."

Thunderstand

[THUN-der-stand] verb

To suddenly understand something not through thinking, but through feeling, the way you know a storm is coming before you see clouds. Understanding that arrives in your body before your mind catches up.

*Etymology: From "thunder" (sudden, **powerful**) + "understand"*

Example: "Watching her daughter struggle with math homework, Carol thunderstood that her own perfectionism was more about her fear than her child's needs."

Unbecause
[un-bih-KAWZ] adverb

Doing something for no reason other than it feels right, without needing to justify or explain the impulse. The opposite of overthinking. Acting from instinct rather **than logic.**

*Etymology: From "un" + "because": action without **required reasoning***

*Example: "Unbecause, Martin turned down the promotion everyone expected him to want, following an inner knowing he couldn't articulate, but **completely trusted.**"*

Veilift
[VAYE-lift] noun

The moment when something you've been trying to understand becomes clear, not through learning more, but through seeing what was always there. Like removing a veil rather than adding information. Often feels like remembering rather **than discovering.**

Etymology: From "veil" + "lift"

*Example: "Reading her grandmother's letters, Anne experienced a profound veilift about love—not learning something new, but recognizing something she'd always known but forgotten how **to see.**"*

Weightlis

[WAYT-liss] adjective

The sensation of dropping a problem you've been carrying for so long, you forgot it wasn't part of your body. Often occurs suddenly and without ceremony, like setting down a heavy bag and remembering what your shoulders feel like when they're not hunched over.

Etymology: From "weight" + "LIS" (laughing in silence vs LOL: laughing out loud) the absence **of burden**

Example: "After five years of trying to make her marriage work, the weightlis feeling of finally accepting it was over surprised Jennifer with its gentleness rather than devastation."

Xenosis

[zen-OH-sis] noun

The realization that you've been living your life according to rules you never actually agreed to. Often followed by the amusing discovery that most of these rules exist only in your own mind and can be quietly abandoned without consequence.

Etymology: From Greek "xenos" (foreign, strange) + **"-osis" (condition)**

Example: "At forty-five, Robert experienced sudden xenosis, realizing he'd been dressing 'professionally' for decades without ever checking if anyone actually cared what he wore."

Yieldful
[YEELD-ful] adjective

The state of being productively receptive rather than actively forcing. Like good soil that grows things not through effort but through allowing. The fertility that comes from stopping resistance.

Etymology: From "yield" + "-ful"

Example: "After months of writer's block, Maria became yieldful, and found that stories began writing themselves through her rather than being wrestled onto the page."

Zephyrness
[ZEF-er-ness] noun

The quality of moving through life with the lightness of a gentle breeze: present but not pushy, effective but not effortful. The art of getting things done without making everything heavy.

*Etymology: From "zephyr" (gentle **wind**) + "-ness"*

*Example: "Watching his grandmother manage the family **crisis with** perfect zephyrness, helping everyone without seeming to try, Marcus realized that strength didn't have to look **like struggle.**"*

Epilogue: A Note from the **Found Dictionary**

These words were discovered written in the margins of discarded dictionaries, on napkins left in coffee shops, and in the notes apps of phones belonging to people who had given up trying to explain feelings that had no names. Each definition represents a moment when someone's inner experience finally found a shape, a sound, or a way to **be shared.**

Language shapes reality. When we name something, we make it possible to recognize it, seek it, and choose it. These words are invitations to notice experiences that may have been happening all along, waiting quietly in the spaces between what we thought we were supposed to feel and what we actually felt.

The dictionary is incomplete, as all dictionaries are. New words are being written every day by people who discover feelings that don't yet have homes in existing vocabularies. The language of inner experience is always evolving, always being invented by those brave enough to pay attention to what's actually happening **inside them.**

If you find yourself living in the territory of an unnamed feeling, consider yourself a cartographer of consciousness. Draw the map. Name the land. Add your word to **the dictionary.**

The missing words are waiting to **be found.**

Usage Notes

Conjugation patterns: Most of these words follow standard English patterns, though many resist being forced into conventional grammatical structures. For example, "thunderstand" cannot be made future tense: you cannot plan to thunderstand something, it **simply happens.**

Regional variations: The word "dolmering" is pronounced differently in various emotional climates. In areas of high social anxiety, it tends to be whispered. In regions of increased self-acceptance, it's spoken with **more confidence.**

Etymology updates: Several words evolved after their initial discovery. "Abeya" was originally "abeya-ing" until speakers realized the experience was too complete to need an **"-ing" ending.**

Pronunciation guide: When in doubt, pronounce these words the way they feel in your body rather than how they look on the page. The correct pronunciation is the one that creates recognition rather than confusion.

Synonyms and antonyms: Most of these words resist traditional synonyms, because they describe experiences for which no previous words existed. Their antonyms are usually not other words, but the absence of the experience itself.

Cultural context: These words emerged from a culture that had created extensive vocabularies for productivity, achievement, and optimization, but had somehow failed to develop language for the equally important experiences of arrival, sufficiency, and peace.

....

Author's Note: This dictionary hack works by giving names to experiences that shape our reality, but often go unrecognized because they lack vocabulary. Once named, these states become easier to access and choose. The act of reading these definitions may create neural pathways that recognize these experiences when they occur naturally, turning unconscious moments of peace into conscious tools for well-being.

*Feel free to invent your own words for experiences that don't yet have names. The dictionary of inner life is always **accepting submissions.***

The Useless Mantra

A Single Page, Revisited

Instructions: Read the following four lines once. Do not memorize them. Do not repeat them. Do not ponder their meaning. Simply let your eyes pass over the words like sunlight through a window, then close this page and forget you ever **saw it.**

....

You are the destination pretending to be the journey.
Happiness is the room you're already sitting in.
You are enough, period.
Stop looking. You are the thing being sought.

....

Warning: These words are designed to be useless. They will not improve you, enlighten you, or solve your problems. They are simply four ways of saying the same obvious thing you already know, but keep forgetting to remember.

Close this book now.

....

*[That's it. The mantra will do whatever it's going to do without **your help**.]*

About the Author

Hanna Kutcher is a walking longitudinal study for 30 years of traditional talk therapy, who dared ask if there's a faster and easier way to figure your s*** out and just love yourself already. Turns out, a little humor and a fresh perspective may be all you need. Find her giving magic carpet rides and expanding consciousness at *Inner Sea Journeys* (innersea.vip).